Joseph: Overcoming Life's Challenges

Discovery Series Bible Study

The football coach was to the point of exasperation: "Losing five games in a row is bad enough. But what really frustrates me is that we keep making the same mistakes over and over. We just aren't learning anything!" Wasting the pain of failure happens off the field as well. We can be slow to learn that what causes the most pain is not the initial loss or hardship but the failure to learn anything in the process.

If we really believe that God is working all things for our good, then one of the great challenges is to allow hard, painful, and tear-filled experiences to be our teacher in the classroom of life. The Old Testament character Joseph learned through extremely difficult circumstances how to overcome. It is my prayer that by examining his life we can learn some important lessons from him.

Bill Crowder for RBC Ministries

Publisher:	RBC Ministries
Editor:	David Sper
Graphic Design:	Alex Soh, Janet Chim, Felix Xu
Cover Photo:	Alex Soh © 2001 RBC Ministries Asia Ltd.
Series Coordinator / Study Guide:	Bill Crowder, Sim Kay Tee

RADIO BIBLE CLASS ~ FOUNDED 1938

ISBN 1-58424-131-4

Table Of Contents

The Lessons Of Life

On the old *Happy Days* television show, Richie Cunningham had just been "grounded for life" by his father, Howard, for misbehavior. As they talked about it, Howard asked his son, "Did you know that there is a lesson in this for you?" Richie's response was priceless: "I figured anything with this much pain had to have a lesson in it somewhere."

That is real life! We do not learn character in times of ease and prosperity, but in times of difficulty. The greatest lessons of life are often the product of our most serious heartaches.

When my father died, a pastor friend came to the funeral home. I had been a pastor only a few months, and my father's funeral would be the first that I would preach. My friend put his arm around my shoulder and said, "I know this hurts an awful lot—and it should. But one day you will be thankful for the lessons you learn this week."

He continued, "I have never lost anyone close to me, but I have preached scores of funerals. Never in those funerals have I felt the ability to truly comfort people in the time of their greatest loss because I have never experienced that pain. What you will learn in your pain will enable you to minister far more effectively to the pain of others."

In one of the most practical books in the New Testament, James wrote these words:

My brethren, count it all joy when you fall into various trials, knowing that the testing of your faith produces patience. But let patience have its perfect work, that you may be perfect and complete, lacking nothing (1:2-4).

His point is simple—God doesn't waste anything! Everything happens in our lives for a reason, and a great part of that reason is to help us grow in our faith.

It has been said that life has to be lived in a forward motion but can only be understood by looking back. This demands that we trust in the loving purposes of a sovereign God. We must trust that He is in control—especially when life seems to be out of control.

> **Joseph can teach us much about how to deal with the tangled threads of our own lives.**

This is what Paul referred to as walking by faith (2 Cor. 5:7). It goes against every element of self-preservation that is ingrained in us. We want to take charge, manipulate, and control. But God wants us to trust in the love of a Father who makes no mistakes. He wants us to rely on the One who makes us "more than conquerors through Him who loved us" (Rom. 8:37).

Such was the life of the Old Testament character Joseph. His life was filled with dark, difficult experiences—yet the final outcome was amazing! In fact, Joseph is able to teach us much about how to deal with the tangled threads of our own lives. He became a godly man in an ungodly culture—a true overcomer—and his example can help prepare us as we face the issues of life.

Overcoming Treachery

There are many beautiful words in the English language—words that are almost musical in their sound. *Treachery* is not one of those words.

When we hear the word *treachery*, we think of Benedict Arnold, who sold out his fledgling nation almost before it was born. We hear Caesar, in anguish from the knife planted firmly in his back, as he cries, *"Et tu, Brute?"* When we hear the word *betrayal*, our minds flash back to a garden on a dark night, the voice of a friend, and a kiss that sold out the Son of God for 30 pieces of silver.

As we enter the life of Joseph, he is standing at the very threshold of treachery—a betrayal that will rise up out of his own family. It will carry with it short-term pain for him, but it is a lesson in overcoming that young Joseph must learn.

The Seedbed For Tension

I remember years ago making a call on a family who had visited our church. As soon as I entered the house, I sensed the tension in the air. It was uncertain whether anyone in the family had love for anyone else, but it was abundantly clear that they did not like one another. In the course of the next 45 minutes, two things became obvious—the husband and wife were far from being on speaking terms with each other, and their personal civil war had migrated from their relationship to their children.

We assume that families will be places of warmth, love, acceptance, and security. But far too often, they don't live up to their billing. They become

7

breeding grounds for anger, resentment, and bitterness. Such was the case with Jacob's household as seen in Genesis 37.

Lighting The Fuse Of Family Anger

The patriarch Jacob, son of Isaac and grandson of Abraham, was learning the hard way that you really do reap what you sow. He had ignored the biblical pattern for marriage in Genesis 2 by taking multiple wives. He had children by these two wives (and their handmaids) and ended up with a mixed family of 12 sons, all vying for position with their father.

The problem was intensified by Jacob's obvious preference for his second wife, Rachel, and her two sons, Joseph and Benjamin. This created serious friction in the family. By being elevated to special status in the household, these two boys became outcasts in their own family.

In addition, Jacob's less-than-sterling character was being reproduced in his sons. His name (Jacob) means "conniver," and Jacob's sons had learned at the feet of the master. The family was riddled with strife, deception, and self-interest. The explosive atmosphere was further destabilized by the poor parenting practices he displayed. Genesis 37 describes three points of potential combustion in the household:

- Jacob used Joseph to spy on the older brothers who hated this "favorite son" (v.2).
- Jacob made a display of his favoritism in the gift of a special tunic (v.3).
- Jacob fed the anger of the sibling rivalry, but their anger was directed at Joseph, not at their father and his foolish actions (v.4).

The growth of conflict between the brothers was rooted in the problems within the marriage. The same results are seen in 1 Samuel 1, where polygamy produced inevitable competition and conflict between the wives. Of course polygamy isn't necessary for conflict to occur. Any breakdown in the husband-wife relationship has serious spillover effects on all the relationships in the home. When that relationship is coupled with misguided parenting that elevates one child above the rest as the object of love and praise, the results can be catastrophic.

By showing preference to Joseph, Jacob made two serious errors. First, he sent wrong signals to Joseph about his position in the family over his older brothers. Second, by inference he inflicted the pain of rejection on the sons who had once been the object of his attention but were now forgotten. The resulting tension created a relational powder keg whose fuse was about to be lit. Jacob's lack of wisdom and obedience had built a family filled with resentment and hate.

> **Any breakdown in the husband-wife relationship**
> **has serious spillover effects on**
> **all the relationships in the home.**

Speaking of family tension, I remember reading an excerpt from a will dated July 1, 1935. It said:

> Unto my two daughters, Frances Marie and Denise Victoria, by reason of their unloving attitudes toward a doting father . . . I leave the sum of $1 each and a father's curse. May their respective lives be filled with misery, unhappiness, and sorrow. May their deaths be soon and of a lingering, torturous nature. May their souls rest in hell and suffer the torments of the damned for eternity.

A family can be a breeding ground for hatred, and the effects can be destructive indeed. Jacob's indiscretions had doused his household with gasoline—and Joseph was about to strike a match!

The Brashness Of Youth

Joseph received a set of dreams that predicted his future rise to greatness. But instead of considering their importance and seeking to understand them, he flaunted them before his family—including the brothers who already hated him. Joseph made three critical errors in judgment:

- He was *indiscriminate*—he didn't recognize the troubled situation in his family.
- He was *insensitive*—he didn't consider the impact of his actions on family members.

- He was *immature*—he didn't stop to think of the hurt that his actions could cause.

The result was that the tension and anger continued to mount. The missing character quality in Joseph's young life was discernment. While it was true that one day he would exercise dominion over his brothers, his actions proved that he wasn't ready for that job yet.

Joseph had to be prepared for the responsibility of leadership, and that preparation would come as he learned the role of a servant. Servant-leadership displays discernment, sensitivity, and maturity. This is true whether it be husbands and their wives, leaders in a church, supervisors with their employees, or civic leaders and citizens. There is a crying need in our generation for leaders with a servant's heart.

For the Christian in leadership, the question is always, "Are you using your position, or are you allowing God to use you in it?" To this end, someone penned what is called "The Leader's Prayer":

Lord, when I'm wrong, make me willing to change. When I'm right, make me easy to live with. So strengthen me that the power of my example will far exceed the authority of my rank.

Joseph had to develop the character of a leader, but it would come only through the lessons and experience of being a servant.

Looking Out For Numbers One Through Ten

In Genesis 37:12-27, Jacob sent Joseph to check on his brothers, and, not surprisingly, these 10 brothers resented Joseph's very presence among them. The pressure escalated as they contemplated "Daddy's Favorite."

First we see that anger had replaced love, even to the point of murder (v.18). And sarcasm had replaced appropriate speech (v.19). Reuben attempted to intervene on Joseph's behalf but was rebuffed (vv.21-22). Finally, the attack took place in several stages:

- They took his coat (v.23), the symbol of their resentment.

- They cast him into a pit (v.24) to remove him from their sight.
- With hardened hearts, they sat down to enjoy a meal while their young brother languished alone in a dark pit (v.25).
- They sold him into slavery (vv.25-28), deciding that making a profit on Joseph's life was the proper end to this sad event.

Notice what the unresolved family tension had produced. The root of bitterness is hate (Mt. 5:21-22). The symptom of bitterness is sarcasm (Jas. 3:1-8). The result of bitterness is manipulation, *using* people instead of *loving* them.

The Root Of Bitterness And Its Tragic Fruit

For those who have studied this biblical story, it is easy to say, "It's okay. Everything will turn out all right in the end." But look at the immediate pain that flowed from a family eaten up with hate. Reuben mourned for Joseph (and his own lack of courage). The brothers lied to their father, but never escaped their personal guilt (see Gen. 42:22). Jacob, the deceiver, was now deceived and he experienced a pain that refused to comforted. He had reaped what he had sown. As he had deceived his father with a goat, he was now deceived by the same means.

The root of bitterness is hate;
the symptom of bitterness is sarcasm;
and the result of bitterness is manipulation.

The last result of this family bitterness was that Joseph was sold into slavery. It's interesting that he is the only one who is not described in the text as being troubled. He was in the best position of them all, because even though he was enslaved he was right where God wanted him. He was right where he had to be so that he could learn the lessons God wanted to teach him—lessons that would one day make him a great leader and enable him to overcome the treachery and betrayal of his own brothers.

Psalm 76:10 says, "Surely the wrath of man shall praise You." Ever faithful, God would take the evil of men in Joseph's life and use it for his good and for His glory.

STUDY
NO. *1*

Overcoming Treachery

Genesis 50:20—"But as for you, you meant evil against me; but God meant it for good, in order to bring it about as it is this day, to save many people alive."

Objective:
To develop a biblical response to mistreatment by others, and to examine our own treatment of other people.

Bible Memorization:
Genesis 50:20

Read:
"Overcoming Treachery" pp.7-11

Warming Up
After reading the descriptions of treachery on page 7, can you identify any other treacherous events in history? What about treachery in your own life?

Thinking Through
On page 5 it says that "We do not learn character in times of ease and prosperity, but in times of difficulty. The greatest lessons of life are often the product of our most serious heartaches." Has this been true in your own experience? Explain your answer.

Jacob's poor parenting created three "points of potential combustion" in his family (p.8). What were they and why were they so dangerous?

Why is it normal to "assume that families will be places of warmth, love, acceptance, and security"? (p.7). How true is this in your own family? Why is the husband-wife relationship critical in setting the tone for the other relationships within the family? (p.8).

Digging In
Key Text: Genesis 37:1-36

In what ways does Joseph's special tunic (Gen. 37:3,23,32) picture the troubled relationships that Joseph has with his parents and brothers? How is it an apt description of Joseph's attitudes toward his family?

This passage contains elements of pride, parental favoritism, envy, hatred, family conflicts, and sibling rivalry. How does it teach us to be alert to these issues? How does it prepare us to respond to betrayal and treachery?

How do you think God was involved in the events of Genesis 37?

Going Further
Refer

According to Romans 5:3-4, James 1:2-4, and 1 Peter 1:6-7, why are trials good for us? What good can come through trials? Do you think these biblical writers are realistic or unrealistic in their perspectives of trials? Why?

Reflect

Consider a situation in which you fell victim to the scheming of a friend, colleague, or family member. How did you feel at the time of betrayal? What good has come out of that situation? What insights from this study can you apply to that experience?

³"And not only that, but we also glory in tribulations, knowing that tribulation produces perseverance; ⁴and perseverance, character; and character, hope."
Romans 5:3-4

²"My brethren, count it all joy when you fall into various trials, ³knowing that the testing of your faith produces patience. ⁴But let patience have its perfect work, that you may be perfect and complete, lacking nothing."
James 1:2-4

⁶"In this you greatly rejoice, though now for a little while, if need be, you have been grieved by various trials, ⁷that the genuineness of your faith, being much more precious than gold that perishes, though it is tested by fire, may be found to praise, honor, and glory at the revelation of Jesus Christ."
1 Peter 1:6-7

Overcoming Temptation

To say that life is filled with trials and temptations is, as sportscaster Howard Cosell used to say, to have "a marvelous grasp of the obvious." To realize, however, that these trials often come on the heels of our greatest successes may be to understand the very essence of what makes life so hard.

It's probably true that how we handle success says as much if not more about us as how we handle failure. In learning to overcome temptation, Joseph was going to be challenged with success and the temptations it brings. And he would demonstrate that the lessons of God were starting to take hold in his young but maturing heart.

In Genesis 39, we see the saga of Joseph's life take a fascinating turn. He had become the property of Potiphar (37:36), an officer of Pharaoh and the captain of the guard. It is here that Joseph, as a servant, would learn how to be a leader—with all of its ups and downs.

The Power Of Testimony

Potiphar was "captain of the guard" (39:1).There is some discussion among Bible scholars as to what that role was. Some say he was a warden, others believe that he was captain of the palace guard, and still others say he was captain of the executioners. What we do know is that Potiphar was wealthy enough to have many servants and slaves (vv.11,14), and he had now added Joseph to his collection. Joseph distinguished himself as a young man of skill and ability, but it became clear that those talents were not the key to his life. Genesis 39:2 gives us the real key: "The Lord was with Joseph." God's presence was the difference.

Imagine how painful it must have been at age 17, not only to have been torn from his family and sold into slavery—but to have his family do it! How easy it would have been to become embittered and hate-filled (like his brothers). But that didn't happen to Joseph. Although he was far from home, the presence of God was very real in his life. In fact, this is the theme of Genesis 39 (see vv.2-3,21,23), and it had a dramatic impact on Potiphar. He could not help but recognize the presence of God in the life of this remarkable slave. Imagine how strong Joseph's testimony had to be for Potiphar, who was a pagan, not only to recognize and admire Joseph's character but to attribute it to God rather than to Joseph.

> ## Trials often come on the heels
> ## of our greatest successes.

The clear implication of the text is that Joseph was not bitter toward his brothers nor enslaved by his circumstances. He was content in the presence of God (cp. Heb. 13:5-6 and Phil. 4:10-13). He didn't mourn his disappointment but became useful where he was. And God used that heart of faithfulness and contentment.

Potiphar recognized God's presence with Joseph (39:3), and he made this young slave the overseer of his entire household (vv.4-6). Joseph now supervised all the other servants, handled public relations, oversaw finances, and was responsible for the provisions for the household (valuable training for a later assignment Joseph would receive).

Everything Joseph touched was blessed. Now, perhaps 10 years after being sold into slavery, Joseph was on top of the world. And now he was more vulnerable than ever to temptation.

The Power Of Temptation

Notice the closing words of Genesis 39:6, "Joseph was handsome in form and appearance." He was good-looking and well-built. Now Potiphar's wife enters the scene. Her response? She "cast longing eyes on Joseph" (v.7). She would have been right at home in modern America. A recent *McCall's* magazine survey polled

60,000 American women, and the results were stunning: 47 percent said that they thought premarital sex was acceptable and 27 percent endorsed extramarital affairs. Potiphar's wife had the same mindset. She was attracted to this young man physically, so she offered herself to him.

Look at Joseph's response. He refused her advances because of a powerful set of convictions. These convictions were not learned from his father, Jacob, nor from his hate-filled brothers, nor in the courts of pagan Egypt. These convictions were learned in the presence of God. He not only battled temptation, but he had a battle plan that he would follow as she continued to pursue him.

He had the right concerns (Gen. 39:8-9)

He was concerned *ethically* that his actions not hurt others, in this case Potiphar. His master had entrusted him with much, and Joseph refused to violate that trust for a moment of pleasure. He also looked beyond the immediate to the ultimate, recognizing the consequences that such sin would have on his relationship with God (v.9). He was concerned *spiritually*, because he understood that all sin is against God. The offer of sensual pleasure is not worth the price tag attached to it.

> **Joseph looked beyond the immediate to the ultimate, recognizing the consequences that such sin would have on his relationship with God.**

He had the right strategy (Gen. 39:10)

He avoided contact with her. Joseph realized that he had to be aware of the lure of sin and avoid its opportunities. He had to be alert!

It's like the story of a man applying for a job as a telegraph operator. One by one the applicants went for their interview, and one by one they were rejected. Finally, it was his turn. As he responded to the interviewer's questions, he was distracted by a tapping sound the man made with his pencil. He alertly translated them into dots and dashes, told the man what he was sending, and was hired for the job.

He had the right escape route (Gen. 39:12)

When Potiphar's wife finally got Joseph alone, he ran as far as he could as fast as he could, leaving his coat behind. What Samson, David, and Solomon did not do, Joseph did. He fled, keeping the courage of his convictions and his integrity intact. He exemplified Paul's advice to Timothy: "Flee . . . youthful lusts" (2 Tim. 2:22). He didn't flirt with sin, argue with it, or reason with it. He fled from it.

In spite of the evil environment, the woman's persistence, and his limited personal spiritual training, Joseph resisted. How?

- He recognized that he belonged to God.
- He recognized sin's effect on others.
- He recognized sin as defiance against God.

This young man's godly character was continuing to be shaped. In a perfect world (or on a 30-minute television sitcom), his commitment would have resulted in everyone living happily ever after. But real life doesn't operate that way. Life in a fallen world seldom rewards right living.

> **Life in a fallen world
> seldom rewards right living.**

The Power Of Revenge

Have you heard of the fury of a woman scorned? Joseph lived it. He was ruled by principles, but she was ruled by passion. And when she was rebuffed, her passions exploded in anger. She had her own strategy—revenge.

- Joseph was lied about to the men of the house (39:13-15)—the second time a coat had been used in a lie about Joseph.
- Joseph was lied about to Potiphar (vv.16-18).
- Joseph was imprisoned again (vv.19-20), and again it was undeserved.

Remember that Potiphar may have been the chief executioner. In ancient Egypt, the penalty for adultery was 1,000 lashes, but the penalty for rape was death. It's possible that Potiphar knew that his wife was lying. At the very least, he knew that such an accusation was out of character for this young man. But desperate to save face, he had to do something. So he imprisoned Joseph.

Joseph ended up in jail for doing the right thing. We protest, "It isn't fair!" And that's true. Often life isn't fair—but our responsibility is to do right and leave the consequences to God.

Now what of Joseph? He responded properly to his enslavement and to his temptation as well. How would he respond to this imprisonment?

Often life isn't fair—
but our responsibility is to do right
and to leave the consequences to God.

The Presence Of God

Once again he found comfort in the presence of his God: "The Lord was with Joseph and showed him mercy" (v.21). It would have been easy to ask, "Why be good and do right if I end up here?" But Joseph didn't. He rested in God's presence, and God blessed him, even in prison (vv.21-23).

Once again, Joseph began to learn what it means to overcome. He was learning from the pains, problems, dangers, and tests of life. All these things come into focus when we view them through the lens of God's sovereign purposes. Then we can trust His will and know His mercy.

Joseph's character was under construction as he was shaped by adversity, punished by men, and honored by God. Genesis 39 ends the way it began—with Joseph in bondage. Yet through it all, his solid faith in God's control had helped him overcome.

Overcoming Temptation

1 Corinthians 10:13—"No temptation has overtaken you except such as is common to man; but God is faithful, who will not allow you to be tempted beyond what you are able, but with the temptation will also make the way of escape, that you may be able to bear it."

Objective:
To embrace contentment with Christ as a strong biblical response to temptation.

Bible Memorization:
1 Corinthians 10:13

Read:
"Overcoming Temptation" pp.15-19

Warming Up

Imagine being torn from your family as a teenager and sold into slavery. In response to such an event, what kind of feelings would flow from your own heart?

Thinking Through

On page 15 we are told that "the Lord was with Joseph." How was God's presence seen, and what was its impact on Potiphar, Joseph's master?

Few things have such a far-reaching impact as the choices we make. On pages 17-18 we see the strategy Joseph chose in order to maintain his own integrity and moral purity. What was this strategy? How could you implement such a strategy in your own life?

Consider the bold quote on page 18: "Life in a fallen world seldom rewards right living." In what ways has life been unfair to you? Can you think of an incident in which you were unjustly penalized or punished for doing the right thing? How did you respond?

Digging In
Key Text: Genesis 39:1-23

What action of God is emphasized in this chapter? Why? What does the phrase "the Lord was with Joseph" (vv.2-3,21,23) mean in practical terms?

What did Potiphar's wife do in her attempts to entice Joseph to sin? (vv.7,10,12). How did Joseph resist in each case?

How would you describe Joseph's inner character? His convictions? His relationship with and devotion to God? What role (if any) do these play in his victory over temptation?

Going Further
Refer
What temptations do you constantly face? Does 1 Corinthians 10:13 encourage or frustrate you in your battle with temptations? Why?

Reflect
What are some of the things that have helped you in your own battles with temptation? (Check all appropriate boxes.) How have these helped?

> ❑ The Word of God
> ❑ Scripture memorization
> ❑ Prayer
> ❑ Fleeing the scene
> ❑ Avoiding the places of temptation
> ❑ Knowing your own limitations and weaknesses
> ❑ Telling a friend about it
> ❑ Other (please describe)

"No temptation has overtaken you except such as is common to man; but God is faithful, who will not allow you to be tempted beyond what you are able, but with the temptation will also make the way of escape, that you may be able to bear it."
1 Corinthians 10:13

Overcoming Disappointment

During his professional baseball career, Joe Torre won batting championships, Gold Glove awards for fielding skill, and World Series titles. Years later, when he was an announcer for the California Angels, he said during a broadcast that earlier in the evening a boy had stopped him with an interesting question. The young man asked Torre, "Did you used to be somebody?" How quickly we forget.

Sometimes we can be swallowed up by the expectation expressed by the question, "What have you done for me lately?" One NFL coach, after a 10-game winning streak, took it further. He said the expectation is no longer "What have you done for me lately?" It's become "What will you do for me next?" How quickly we forget.

Does Anyone Remember?

It would certainly be understandable if Joseph had lapsed into self-pity at this point. He was imprisoned and treated harshly. Psalm 105:18 says of Joseph, "They hurt his feet with fetters, he was laid in irons." All this for the crime of honoring his master and maintaining sexual purity.

But the Lord was still with him, and Joseph rose to a position of leadership—even in prison. God gave him favor with the jailer (39:21), and the jailer entrusted everything under his authority to Joseph's care. Why? "Because the Lord was with [Joseph]; and whatever he did, the Lord made it prosper" (v.23).

Joseph was still learning the lessons of leadership. And one of the lessons that is critical to the matter of overcoming is the lesson of patience. Though Joseph was unjustly imprisoned again, he went about the business of being useful where he was. He faithfully served and patiently waited because he was learning that he was not there by accident. He was not forgotten. God not only remembered, but He had a plan for Joseph that included a tour of duty in the prison of Egypt.

The God Who Never Forgets

Joseph was in prison for a divine appointment. In Genesis 40:1, the pieces of the puzzle begin to come together. Two of Pharaoh's officials—his royal butler and his royal baker—offended their ruler. These were not just household servants. In ancient times of palace intrigue and political assassinations, it was absolutely critical that these men be totally loyal. Somehow they had failed Pharaoh, so they were placed in the prison where Joseph was the head steward (vv.2-3).

Notice who entrusted them to Joseph's care. It was the captain of the guard—Potiphar (v.4; cp. 37:36). Joseph accepted the responsibility and began the task of serving these disgraced members of Pharaoh's court. This was not just some cosmic accident. It was a divine appointment. How necessary it is that we see this and embrace it. There is no such thing as a coincidence. God is in control of our lives. Nothing happens by accident. Everything occurs for a purpose.

> **God is in control of our lives.**
> **Nothing happens by accident.**

When I was in college, I was faced with a dilemma. I was on the soccer team, but I was also involved in a traveling ministry. A scheduling conflict arose between the two activities. Both had events that I was committed to, and I had to choose between them. I chose the soccer game and began making arrangements for a substitute for the traveling ministry team. On the day before these conflicting events, I was injured in a soccer game and forbidden to play in the next game. Quickly, I reversed course, and went with the traveling ministry team. On the day that I would have been playing soccer, I met the young woman who would later become my wife! After the fact, I learned that she had been a last-minute substitute on the trip. We met our life partners on a trip that, humanly speaking, neither of us was supposed to be on.

One of the great joys—and challenges—of life is to look expectantly for the hand of God in all of life's circumstances. Joseph and these two fallen royal officials converged in prison right on schedule for the perfect plan of God—though they certainly wouldn't have chosen those circumstances for themselves.

> **One of the great joys—and challenges— of life is to look expectantly for the hand of God in all of life's circumstances.**

Lest We Forget

Don't miss this. In spite of (or perhaps because of) his own difficulty and hardship, Joseph had become sensitive to others, a quality that he previously lacked (Gen. 37). He looked at these men (40:6-7), and recognized their hurt and distress. How easy it would have been to turn away, thinking, "No one is caring about the mistreatment I have received. Why should I care about anyone else's?" But he didn't. Joseph's response to the disappointment of unjust imprisonment was twofold:

- *Vertical*—he didn't allow his circumstances to disrupt his relationship with God.
- *Horizontal*—he didn't allow his hurt to prevent him from caring about the hurts of others.

Joseph could have ignored them, but he didn't. He had the grace to set aside his personal adversity and help others who were hurting. Life is filled with disappointment and loss, but we can be overcomers by refusing to become self-absorbed and self-centered. Instead of wasting our energy in self-pity, we can invest our time in meeting the needs of others.

For example, a missionary couple in India saw their six children killed, so they raised 300 foster children. Following the tragic flood at Toccoa Falls, Georgia, a man whose wife and two children had died in the flood said, "Every time I wanted to cry, someone else needed help and I felt compelled to offer. I was so consumed with helping others that I had no time to worry about myself."

Is that how you respond to adversity and disappointment? Or do you become so consumed with your own pain that you are blind to the pain of others? Sensitivity to the needs of others can be deadened by preoccupation with personal disappointment. But that wasn't true of Joseph. He not only noticed and cared—he got involved.

Forget Me Not

Joseph interpreted the dreams of the two officials (vv.8-19), making sure they knew that he was not the one who deserved the credit—but God. It's a notable contrast to chapter 37, when he lorded his dreams over his brothers. Now his trust was in the Lord, not in himself. After Joseph interpreted the butler's dream, he asked only that he would not forget him (40:14-15).

Three days later, both dreams were fulfilled—exactly as Joseph had interpreted them (vv.20-22). Once again Joseph had set aside personal gain. And once again he had refused the path of selfishness. His care and concern for these men was marvelous in its expression of true humility and godly character.

And how was that sensitivity rewarded? "The chief butler did not remember Joseph, but forgot him" (40:23). Earlier, Joseph's purity was rewarded with imprisonment. Now his caring was paid back with insensitivity. And notice for how long—2 full years (41:1).

Joseph was abandoned—this time by a friend, not an enemy, and for a long time, not a short one. It would have been easy for him to succumb to disillusionment and disappointment. But those are the results of putting our trust in men—and Joseph's trust was in the Lord. Even though the butler had forgotten Joseph, God hadn't. These are the times that build into us the indispensable character quality of patient trust. James 1:2-4 says that this can be learned only through trials. James teaches that without patience there will be no maturity, and without trials, delays, and disappointments there will be no patience. It has been said that a man is not a hero because he is braver than anyone else but because he is brave longer.

Joseph had overcome treachery, temptation, and now, disappointment. The lessons of becoming an overcomer were taking shape in his life—and he was finally ready for God to use him in a special way.

STUDY NO. 3

Overcoming Disappointment

Romans 8:28—"And we know that all things work together for good to those who love God, to those who are the called according to His purpose."

Objective:

To examine our response when disappointed by others, and to understand the value of those difficult experiences.

Bible Memorization:

Romans 8:28

Read:

"Overcoming Disappointment" pp.22-25

Warming Up
One of the greatest challenges of life is the challenge to learn patience. Why is this virtue such a struggle for so many of us?

Thinking Through
On page 23 we are told, "One of the lessons that is critical to the matter of overcoming is the lesson of patience." Why is patience so important to being a good leader? How did Joseph display his growth in the character quality of patience?

Consider the bold quote from page 23: "God is in control of our lives. Nothing happens by accident." Do you agree or disagree with this very sweeping, comprehensive statement? Support your view with Scripture.

Joseph is described as having a twofold response to the disappointment of his unjust imprisonment (p.24). What were the elements of that response, and how did he seek to live them out? How did these responses impact his relationships?

Digging In
Key Text: Genesis 40:1-23
What was Joseph's analysis of his own present circumstances? (Gen. 40:14-15). What emotions

(anger, sadness, bitterness, despondency, etc.) do you think Joseph would have had to deal with even as he described his situation?

What did Joseph expect the cupbearer to do for him? (Gen 40:14). How do you think Joseph's faith was affected when the cupbearer failed to remember him? (Gen. 40:15,23).

Do you think that Joseph was disappointed with God when he saw that the dreams of the cupbearer and the baker were fulfilled so quickly (Gen. 40:20-22) though his own dream (Gen. 37) had remained unfulfilled for several years? Why or why not?

Going Further
Refer
Joseph becomes a great model to us of spiritual patience. Can you identify other Bible characters who displayed patience? Can you identify characters whose lives displayed impatience?

Reflect
When you respond to life's difficulties impatiently, it tends to affect those around you in a harmful way. Can you remember a time when your impatience hurt someone you care about? Have you resolved the resulting hurt? If so, how? If not, will you commit to do it soon?

[14]"Remember me when it is well with you, and please show kindness to me; make mention of me to Pharaoh, and get me out of this house. [15]For indeed I was stolen away from the land of the Hebrews; and also I have done nothing here that they should put me into the dungeon."
Genesis 40:14-15

[20]"Now it came to pass on the third day, which was Pharaoh's birthday, that he made a feast for all his servants; and he lifted up the head of the chief butler and of the chief baker among his servants. [21]Then he restored the chief butler to his butlership again, and he placed the cup in Pharaoh's hand. [22]But he hanged the chief baker, as Joseph had interpreted to them. [23]Yet the chief butler did not remember Joseph, but forgot him."
Genesis 40:20-23

Overcoming Success

Years ago, Erwin Lutzer wrote a very helpful little book titled *Failure: The Back Door To Success*. It could have been written about Joseph. Many times, it takes years of failures and setbacks to become an "overnight success."

Abraham Lincoln is a classic example. He had two failed businesses, one nervous breakdown, endured the death of a sweetheart, and was defeated for public office no less than 10 times over the space of almost 30 years. Then, incredibly, he was elected President of the United States. Years of failure had equipped him to deal with the heady air of the heights of power.

Those repeated reversals, apparent failures, and personal tragedies did not defeat Lincoln. They strengthened his character and commitment. So it was with Joseph. After 13 years of reversals, failure, and tragedy, the light of day finally entered his cell. He had been forgotten by the royal butler for 2 full years. It was 2 years of continued suffering, pain, and solitude. But it was also 2 years of preparation and character development. Now the time for which Joseph had been prepared had arrived. In God's perfect timing, Genesis 41 records what happened as the servant and the task converged in a moment in time.

Dreams You Would Like To Forget

The stage was set by a pair of dreams that Pharaoh experienced (41:1-8). These dreams spoke of a coming calamity for the nation, but their message was unclear and he was troubled by the uncertainty of them. Like the butler and baker 2 years before, Pharaoh sensed that these were beyond ordinary dreams. So he sought the wisest men of his kingdom to interpret them.

This exposes a significant principle in our spiritual living. Pharaoh was troubled by spiritual things that were beyond his grasp. But there was great danger in seeking spiritual answers in the wrong places. His wise men and magicians didn't know the God who was dealing with him, and their answers were inadequate for the turmoil in his heart.

There is a great spiritual hunger today. And into the vacuum of spiritual truth come cultists, false teachers, and false spiritual leaders who find that people's hunger makes them easy prey for eartickling deception.

Answers must be sought from God's revealed truth. The empty answers of false teachers are void of the necessary power to address true spiritual needs or answer the burning spiritual questions of the human heart. Until we are willing to accept the authority of God's truth in our lives, we will not have the answers we need for the things that trouble our hearts and minds.

A Dream Remembered

In the pressure of the failures of Pharaoh's wisemen to interpret the dreams, the butler remembered someone who had succeeded (40:9-13). He recounted to Pharaoh the prison dreams and the accurate interpretation he had received from a Hebrew prisoner there. Now Joseph would come into contact with the third in a trilogy of "dream pairs"—all linked together.

- Dreams of dominion over his brothers.
- Dreams of the butler and the baker.
- Dreams of the grain and the cows.

It's amazing how these dreams fit together. The second pair of dreams put Joseph in contact with the third set of dreams, which then enabled the fulfillment of the first set of dreams. The promises God made to Joseph 13 years earlier had now come full circle. To the eyes of men, it may appear about 13 years late in arriving. But in the sovereign plan of God it was right on time.

A Dream Come True

Pharaoh was out of options, so he called for Joseph. With Joseph's liberation (41:14-16) we see a second vital principle—godly character is unaffected by the harsh circumstances of life. Undiminished by unfair treatment and years in prison,

29

Joseph stepped forward with three evident qualities:

Dignity—"He shaved" (Egyptians were clean shaven) and he "changed his clothing" (v.14). Joseph dressed in appropriate clothes to come before the king. He had a sense of propriety and decorum that years in prison could not erase.

Humility—"It is not in me" (v.16). Joseph didn't use the situation for self-promotion. He didn't try to exalt himself as he had earlier in his life (Gen. 37:5-10). Through all that had happened, he learned to put his trust in the Lord, not in himself. As Scottish theologian James Denney (1856–1917) said, "No man can at the same time prove that he is clever and that Jesus Christ is mighty to save."

Faith—"God will give Pharaoh an answer" (v.16). Sounds like something Daniel (2:27-30) and Paul (Acts 26) would say in the future. Joseph expressed his faith and gave the glory to God. This must have seemed unusual coming from a prisoner and slave.

God's patient investment in the life of Joseph was now paying dividends. These first words spoken by Joseph after prison revealed that the lessons had been well learned.

A Dreamweaver At Work

Pharaoh told Joseph his dream (41:17-36). The failure of Pharaoh's wisest men set the stage for God's glory to be revealed through a common slave. What was beyond human reason was not beyond the all-knowing God.

The answer to the dreams? "God has shown Pharaoh what He is about to do" (v.25). Joseph had learned that he could rest in the sovereignty of God. The double dream was confirmed and would be fulfilled because God is God. The ultimate lesson Joseph had learned through slavery, imprisonment, and mistreatment was that God is in control. He will do what He says, for He is in charge.

Joseph challenged Pharaoh to see the purposes of God and to plan accordingly—because if God said it, it would happen. Joseph boldly offered counsel to the ruler of the land, and it was wise counsel indeed. He told him to plan for the lean years by being frugal during the plentiful years. Joseph had proven the benefit of his training by seeing the need and responding to it wisely. As Gladstone said, "A great statesman is a man who knows the direction God is going for the next 50 years!" Joseph did—when no one else had a clue.

The Dream Answered

Pharaoh made a decision that would change the ancient world. He appointed Joseph to oversee the food supplies of all of Egypt. Why? Because he saw in Joseph the single most important characteristic of a true leader. He was "a man in whom is the Spirit of God" (v.38).

This gives us yet another principle to consider: The qualifications of a true leader are not merely physical, they are spiritual. It is not just about talent or skill but about character and relationship with God. The key character qualities of a great leader (which took years of suffering to build into Joseph) are internal, not external. They deal with knowing God, not with being great.

Once again God's timing was perfect. Two years earlier, Joseph's ability to interpret dreams would have been a novelty. Now, it was a national treasure. Joseph was raised to the position God had promised so many years before. He was exalted over all Pharaoh's house (vv.40-45) and was ready to face and overcome the great tests that success brings to a leader. He was ready for:

- **Perseverance**—It would not be easy for a Hebrew to rule Egypt. The pressure would be intense, especially as the famine wore on.
- **Performance**—The skills Joseph had learned in small duties would now be applied to a major task.
- **Pride**—J. Oswald Sanders wrote, "Not every man can carry a full cup. Sudden elevation frequently leads to pride and a fall. The most exacting test of all is to survive prosperity."

But Joseph was ready for the pressure and the responsibility. He would overcome because God had prepared him. As Samuel Rutherford said, "Praise God for the hammer, the file, and the furnace. The hammer molds us, the file sharpens us, and the fire tempers us." Joseph experienced it all, and he was ready to be used of God.

STUDY
NO **4**

Overcoming
Success

James 1:2-4—"My
brethren, count it all joy
when you fall into various
trials, knowing that the
testing of your faith
produces patience. But let
patience have its perfect
work, that you may be
perfect and complete,
lacking nothing."

Objective:
**To see the need
for dependence
on God in times of
success, as well as
in times of failure.**

Bible Memorization:
James 1:2-4

Read:
**"Overcoming
Success"
pp.28-31**

Warming Up
Which is more difficult to handle—failure or success?
Which one poses a greater threat to the Christian?
Why?

Thinking Through
On page 29 we are told that Pharaoh faced great
spiritual danger by seeking spiritual answers in the
wrong places. What were those wrong places? What
would be their equivalent in our culture?

What three qualities show that Joseph's godly
character had not been diminished by his harsh
and unfair treatment in prison? (p.30). Why is each
one significant?

What were the three great tests of success that
Joseph would encounter after being elevated to a
position of prominence in Pharaoh's court? (p.31).
Why was Joseph prepared to take on each of these
challenges?

Digging In
Key Text: Genesis 41:1-57
How many times and in what different ways does
Joseph acknowledge God in this chapter? What does
this say about the sovereignty of God and the
humility of Joseph?

Pharaoh appointed Joseph to the second highest-ranking position in Egypt (Gen. 41:41-44). What dangers and temptations do you think Joseph would have to face and overcome in this role?

Pharaoh said to Joseph, "Inasmuch as God has shown you all this, there is no one as discerning and wise as you" (Gen. 41:39). The Joseph in Genesis 41 is very different from the Joseph of Genesis 37. What transformation took place in Joseph's life? How did the 13 years of betrayal, hardships, trials, disappointments, humiliation, and prison contribute to making Joseph into such a man?

Going Further

Refer

Joseph told Pharaoh that God would give him "an answer of peace" (Gen 41:16). How is peace that recognizes the control of God over life's failures and successes produced in one's heart? What biblical texts reinforce this idea?

Reflect

On page 31, Samuel Rutherford is quoted as saying, "Praise God for the hammer, the file, and the furnace. The hammer molds us, the file sharpens us, and the fire tempers us." Joseph experienced it all, and he was ready to be used of God. What have been God's hammer, file, and fire in your life—and what have they prepared you for?

---

[15] "And Pharaoh said to Joseph, 'I have had a dream, and there is no one who can interpret it. But I have heard it said of you that you can understand a dream, to interpret it.' [16] So Joseph answered Pharaoh, saying, 'It is not in me; God will give Pharaoh an answer of peace.'"
Genesis 41:15-16

"Then Joseph said to Pharaoh, 'The dreams of Pharaoh are one; God has shown Pharaoh what He is about to do.'"
Genesis 41:25

"Then Pharaoh said to Joseph, 'Inasmuch as God has shown you all this, there is no one as discerning and wise as you.'"
Genesis 41:39

Overcoming Bitterness

At the Nuremberg War Crimes trials following World War II, one of the defendants, on hearing the charges against him, responded to the prosecutor, "It is your word against mine." The prosecutor's answer was profound: "No, it's your word against the victim's. He survived and is prepared to testify against you."

In Joseph's story, it's certainly hard to visualize him as a victim at this point, isn't it? He was now the second most powerful man on earth, and he had absolute control over the destinies of millions of people—including the brothers who had sold him into slavery so many years earlier.

Much had happened since Joseph rose to power (Gen. 41). The 7 years of plenty predicted by Pharaoh's dreams had come and gone—and Joseph's plan had worked to perfection. The grain was stored, and now, in the midst of the 7 years of famine, the world was coming to Pharaoh's (and to Joseph's) doorstep for food. In Genesis 42, Joseph's brothers came seeking food, and he provided it for them.

In the course of that meeting, he questioned them and discovered that their father and younger brother were still alive. Joseph then began to set the wheels in motion for a reunion. He sensed that his brothers had changed—but for the sake of Benjamin, he had to make sure. In the ensuing events, he forced them to return with Benjamin. Then he prepared for the final test. At the banquet referred to in chapter 43, he gave Benjamin five times more than the other brothers, and they didn't resent the kind of favoritism that they had despised so viciously in Joseph. Then he seemed to put Benjamin in harm's way to test them.

Would they protect Benjamin, or abandon him as they had abandoned Joseph 20 years earlier?

Only God can look at the heart (1 Sam. 16:7), so Joseph put in motion the test that would expose them and reveal how genuine their apparent change really was.

A Plan For The Test (44:1-13)

After the feast, Joseph commanded his butler to do several things: Fill their sacks with food, return their money, and put his silver cup in Benjamin's bag.

Why? The only way Joseph could test their character was to "return to the scene of the crime." They had to be put in the position of choosing between rescuing Benjamin at great personal risk, or abandoning him to slavery for personal gain.

As soon as the brothers departed for Canaan, Joseph sent his servants to catch them and accuse them of the theft of the cup. The brothers reacted with shock and confusion. They claimed honesty based on the return of money they had found in their bags on the first trip for food. And they backed up their claims of honesty with a bold offer: "Kill the guilty one, and enslave the rest!"

The extreme nature of their offer was intended to prove their innocence and sincerity. They would certainly not make such an offer if even one of them was guilty. The steward's reply in verse 10 raised the stakes—and the pressure: "Only the guilty will be enslaved." Imagine the mounting tension as one by one the sacks were examined, and one by one found to contain only grain. The steward moved from elder to younger, and the stress of the moment reached its peak as they finally arrived at Benjamin's donkey.

Imagine the shock and pain as the cup was found in his sack. How could it be? They were so certain of their innocence. How would they respond? "Then they tore their clothes" (v.13). They had reaped what they had sown, and in this dramatic gesture of mourning they displayed the depth of their grief and despair. They responded to Benjamin's distress the same way Jacob had responded years before when shown the bloody coat of colors that had belonged to Joseph.

Now the $64,000 question had to be answered. The agreement was that only the guilty would be enslaved and the rest could go home. The easy thing to do would be to leave Benjamin and go home. But they didn't. Envy and resentment no longer governed their thoughts and deeds. They returned with Benjamin, determined that whatever was to be faced they would face together. The evidence was there. They were truly changed men.

A Plea For Mercy (44:14-34)

Notice the difference in their attitudes from years before:

- "They fell before [Joseph] on the ground" (v.14), fulfilling the promise of Joseph's first set of dreams.
- "How shall we clear ourselves? God has found out the iniquity of your servants" (v.16). There were no excuses or rationalizations. There was no attempt to cover up. They admitted, through Judah, their guilt and submitted to slavery as a group. It was "we," not "he." Joseph tested them further with an offer of release, and they passed with flying colors.
- "Let [me] remain instead of the lad" (vv.33-34). What a turnabout. The same Judah who had led in the plan to sell Joseph offered to be Benjamin's substitute as a slave in Egypt. Why? Out of concern for their father (vv.19-32). He openly acknowledged that the young man was now Jacob's favorite. But instead of resenting this favorite-son status, he longed to preserve it by giving himself.

Jesus said, "By their fruits you will know them" (Mt. 7:20), and the change in Judah was real. We have been examining God's work in the life of Joseph, but God had also been working in Judah and his brothers.

A Passionate Reunion (45:1-15)

For Joseph, the years of pain dissolved in a moment of joy, and he wept uncontrollably in the presence of his brothers. They were tears of joy because his brothers had truly changed, and tears of love because at last they were as brothers should be.

The room was electric as Joseph finally said the words that he had longed to say since he first saw them coming for food: "I am Joseph" (v.3). But they were terrified. The dream had come true. Joseph had the power of life and death over them. What would he do? Notice his tenderness toward them:

- "He wept aloud" (v.2), openly expressing his emotion.
- "Please come near to me" (v.4). They had been apart far too long.
- "Do not . . . be grieved or angry with yourselves" (v.5). This was a time for joy.
- "God sent me" (vv.5,7-8). They were to trust that God was in control.
- "Go . . . and bring my father" (vv.9,13). It was time to share the joy.

Forgiveness resolved the issue of guilt. Merrill Unger wrote, "Joseph displayed his deep faith in the omnipotence of God—overriding Satan, demonic powers, and wicked men to work out His sovereign will and unfrustratable plan. Faith lifted the whole sordid crime out of the pit of misery and self-recrimination and placed it on the mountain peak of divine sovereignty where God's forgiving grace not only heals but wipes away the past and the pain" (*Unger's Commentary On The Old Testament*, Moody Press, 1981, p.94).

Joseph had overcome all these things—particularly the potential bitterness that would have seemed so normal. He exemplified grace, giving full forgiveness and no revenge. He exemplified love, discarding the wrongs of the past for the compassion of the present. He exemplified faith, trusting that God would preserve him from the bitterness that leads to self-destruction.

I was deeply moved when I read about Mr. and Mrs. Robert Bristol of Dearborn, Michigan. They traveled on their vacation to San Diego for the purpose of sharing Christ with a man in prison. The thing that made it so amazing was that this criminal was in jail for raping and murdering their precious daughter. That is a spirit of mercy born out of grace. It is full love that was not born out of ease or comfort or convenience, but out of suffering and hardship.

That is the only way to overcome bitterness. When we trust God and rest in Him, we can love others. Why? Because we believe in a God who is big enough to work in all things for our good.

STUDY NO. **5**

Overcoming Bitterness

Ephesians 4:31-32—"Let all bitterness, wrath, anger, clamor, and evil speaking be put away from you, with all malice. And be kind to one another, tenderhearted, forgiving one another, even as God in Christ forgave you."

Objective:
To gain victory over bitterness by the power of forgiveness.

Bible Memorization:
Ephesians 4:31-32

Read:
"Overcoming Bitterness" pp.34-37

Warming Up
Have you ever known a truly bitter person? What do you think was at the heart of that person's bitterness? What were the results of the bitterness?

Thinking Through
How did Joseph get his brothers to, in a sense, "return to the scene of the crime"? (p.35). Why was this important? How did their choice between self-preservation and self-sacrifice reveal the change in their hearts?

Notice the brothers' responses to Benjamin's dilemma (p.36). What does it say about the guilt they had carried for their mistreatment of Joseph?

On page 37 it says, "Forgiveness resolved the issue of guilt." Why is forgiveness the only real remedy for broken relationships and the only real escape from the grip of bitterness?

Digging In
Key Text: Genesis 50:20
In the context of this verse, the brothers feared retaliation by Joseph following their father's death. Why do their words in Genesis 50:16-17 bring Joseph to tears?

In verse 20, Joseph acknowledged a balance between God's sovereignty and man's responsibility. How is that balance revealed? Is it a balance you can explain? Why or why not?

Joseph responded to their words of fear with words of comfort and kindness (v.21). How does this response mirror the character of Christ? The character of the Christian?

Going Further
Refer
According to Colossians 3:12-14, what attitudes and virtues are to be characteristic of a Christian who is in conflict with another believer?

Reflect
Consider the relationships in your life. Are there matters of resentment, anger, hurt, or mistreatment that have disrupted those relationships? Joseph's example teaches us that forgiveness is the only meaningful solution to those issues. What steps will you take to reconcile with those who have hurt you?

[20] "'But as for you, you meant evil against me; but God meant it for good, in order to bring it about as it is this day, to save many people alive. [21] Now therefore, do not be afraid; I will provide for you and your little ones.' And he comforted them and spoke kindly to them."
Genesis 50:20-21

[12] "Therefore, as the elect of God, holy and beloved, put on tender mercies, kindness, humility, meekness, longsuffering; [13] bearing with one another, and forgiving one another, if anyone has a complaint against another; even as Christ forgave you, so you also must do. [14] But above all these things put on love, which is the bond of perfection."
Colossians 3:12-14

The Trust That Overcomes

In Genesis 50:20, we read Joseph's final words to his brothers. They are a capsule of his life's view: "As for you, you meant evil against me; but God meant it for good, in order to bring it about as it is this day, to save many people alive." This amazing perspective reflected a life that had embraced the living God and trusted Him completely.

As you face the pains and heartaches and mistreatments of life, it is only by complete confidence in the goodness and plan of God that you can overcome. The things that could destroy you can become building blocks on the journey of faith as you look for the hand of God in all the circumstances of life. "This is the victory that has overcome the world—our faith" (1 Jn. 5:4).

If you have never confessed your sin and trusted Jesus Christ as your Lord and Savior, life can be a jumbled ball of confusion. But the One who died for your sins and gave Himself for your failures can bring rightness with God, forgiveness of sin, and a new sense of wholeness and purpose into your weary soul. Christ came into the world because of His love for you, and that love can bring an end to the emptiness or bitterness or sinfulness that wracks your life.

Accept by faith the gift of eternal life and personal forgiveness He offers, for the only way to really overcome forever is to accept the victory of Calvary that He accomplished for you. "The gift of God is eternal life in Christ Jesus our Lord" (Rom. 6:23). Now that is real victory—and real overcoming.

Discovery Series Bible Study Leader's And User's Guide

Statement Of Purpose

The *Discovery Series Bible Study* (DSBS) series provides assistance to pastors and leaders in discipling and teaching Christians through the use of RBC Ministries *Discovery Series* booklets. The DSBS series uses the inductive Bible-study method to help Christians understand the Bible more clearly.

Study Helps

Listed at the beginning of each study are the key verse, objective, and memorization verses. These will act as the compass and map for each study.

Some key Bible passages are printed out fully. This will help the students to focus on these passages and to examine and compare the Bible texts more easily—leading to a better understanding of their meanings. Serious students are encouraged to open their own Bible to examine the other Scriptures as well.

How To Use DSBS (for individuals and small groups)

Individuals—Personal Study
- Read the designated pages of the book.
- Carefully consider and answer all the questions.

Small Groups—Bible-Study Discussion
- To maximize the value of the time spent together, each member should do the lesson work prior to the group meeting.
- Recommended discussion time: 45–55 minutes.
- Engage the group in a discussion of the questions, seeking full participation from each of the members.

Overview Of Lessons

Study	Topic	Bible Text	Reading	Questions
1	Overcoming Treachery	Gen. 37:1-36	pp.7-11	pp.12-13
2	Overcoming Temptation	Gen. 39:1-23	pp.15-19	pp.20-21
3	Overcoming Disappointment	Gen. 40:1-23	pp.22-25	pp.26-27
4	Overcoming Success	Gen. 41:1-57	pp.28-31	pp.32-33
5	Overcoming Bitterness	Gen. 50:20	pp.34-37	pp.38-39

The DSBS format incorporates a "layered" approach to Bible study that includes four segments. These segments form a series of perspectives that become increasingly more personalized and focused. These segments are:

Warming Up. In this section, a general interest question is used to begin the discussion (in small groups) or "to get the juices flowing" (in personal study). It is intended to begin the process of interaction at the broadest, most general level.

Thinking Through. Here, the student or group is invited to interact with the *Discovery Series* material that has been read. In considering the information and implications of the booklet, these questions help to drive home the critical concepts of that portion of the booklet.

Digging In. Moving away from the *Discovery Series* material, this section isolates a key biblical text from the manuscript and engages the student or group in a brief inductive study of that passage of Scripture. This brings the authority of the Bible into the forefront of the study as we consider its message to our hearts and lives.

Going Further. This final segment contains two parts. In *Refer*, the student or group has the opportunity to test the ideas of the lesson against the rest of the Bible by cross-referencing the text with other verses. In *Reflect*, the student or group is challenged to personally apply the lesson by making a practical response to what has been learned.

Pulpit Sermon Series (for pastors and church leaders)

Although the *Discovery Series Bible Study* is primarily for personal and group study, pastors may want to use this material as the foundation for a series of messages on this important issue. The suggested topics and their corresponding texts are as follows:

Sermon No.	Topic	Text
1	Overcoming Treachery	Gen. 37:1-36
2	Overcoming Temptation	Gen. 39:1-23
3	Overcoming Disappointment	Gen. 40:1-23
4	Overcoming Success	Gen. 41:1-45
5	Overcoming Bitterness	Gen. 50:20

Final Thoughts

The DSBS will provide an opportunity for growth and ministry. To internalize the spiritual truths of each study in a variety of environments, the material is arranged to allow for flexibility in the application of the truths discussed.

Whether DSBS is used in small-group Bible studies, adult Sunday school classes, adult Bible fellowships, men's and women's study groups, or church-wide applications, the key to the strength of the discussion will be found in the preparation of each participant. Likewise, the effectiveness of personal and pastoral use of this material will be directly related to the time committed to using this resource.

As you use, teach, or study this material, may you "grow in the grace and knowledge of our Lord and Savior Jesus Christ" (2 Pet. 3:18).

Reflections

Reflections

Reflections

Our Daily Bread

You can begin to receive *Our Daily Bread* at your home or your office. Just mail us this request form today! We'd love to welcome you as a regular member of RBC Ministries.

Once you are a member, you will receive:

Our Daily Bread: Daily devotional articles that will challenge and inspire you as you spend time in God's Word.

Discovery Series: Bible study booklets providing insight to a variety of subjects for people eager to apply God's Word to their lives. We will send you one title with *Our Daily Bread* each quarter.

☐ **Yes!** I want to become a member of RBC Ministries and receive *Our Daily Bread* regularly.

Send me: (Quarterly) ☐ English ODB
☐ Simplified Chinese ODB
☐ Traditional Chinese ODB

Please print clearly in block letters:

Full Name:_____

Address: _____

_____

Postcode:_____ Tel: _____

Church:_____ E-Mail: _____

Occupation: _____ Date of Birth:_____

Support for RBC Ministries comes from the gifts of our members and friends.

Please refer to page 48 for RBC offices near you.

RBC Ministries Offices
Please direct all correspondence to the office nearest you:

Headquarters
RBC Ministries - Grand Rapids MI 49555-0001 USA
Telephone: (+1-616) 954-1292 Fax: (+1-616) 957-5741 Email: imo@rbc.org

Africa-Asia Region
Kenya — RBC Ministries Kenya - PO Box 2761 City Square 00200 Kenya
Telephone: (+254-2) 374-9655 Fax: (+254-2) 374-0721 Email: kenya@rbc.org

Nigeria — RBC Ministries Nigeria - PO Box 8132 Ikeja Lagos State Nigeria
Telephone: (+234-1) 493-8243 Email: nigeria@rbc.org

South Africa — RBC Ministries South Africa - PO Box 12221 Hatfield 0028 South Africa
Telephone: (+27-12) 344-5875 Fax: (+27-12) 344-5878 Email: southafrica@rbc.org

Sri Lanka (Regional Office) — RBC Ministries Lanka - PO Box 19 Dehiwala 10350 Sri Lanka
Telephone: (+94-74) 201-694 Fax: (+94-1) 719-766 Email: lanka@rbc.org

Zimbabwe — RBC Ministries Zimbabwe - PO Box EH301 Emerald Hill Harare Zimbabwe
Fax: (+263-4) 333-028 Email: zimbabwe@rbc.org

Asia-Pacific Region
Australia — RBC Ministries South Pacific Ltd - PO Box 3052 Mandurah East WA 6210 Australia
Telephone: (+61-8) 9581-7882 Fax: (+61-8) 9581-9221 Email: australia@rbc.org

Hong Kong — RBC Ministries Ltd - Kowloon Central PO Box 74025 Kowloon Hong Kong
Telephone: (+852) 2626-1102 Fax: (+852) 2626-0216 Email: hongkong@rbc.org

Indonesia — RBC Indonesia - PO Box 2500 Jakarta 11025 Indonesia
Telephone: (+62-21) 544-2152 Fax: (+62-21) 2561 0013 Email: indonesia@rbc.org

Japan — RBC Ministries Japan - PO Box 46 Ikoma Nara-ken Japan 630-0291
Telephone: (+81-743) 75-8230 Fax: (+81-743) 75-8299 Email: japan@rbc.org

Malaysia — RBC Resources Sdn Bhd - PO Box 86 Taman Sri Tebrau 80057 Johor Bahru Malaysia
Telephone: (+060-7) 335-5919 Fax: (+060-7) 335-7828 Email: malaysia@rbc.org

New Zealand — RBC Ministries New Zealand - PO Box 1693 Paraparaumu Beach Kapiti Coast 6450 New Zealand
Telephone: (+64-4) 902-5637 Fax: (+64-4) 902-5638 Email: newzealand@rbc.org

Singapore (Regional office) — RBC Ministries Asia Ltd - Geylang Post Office PO Box 15 Singapore 913801
Telephone: (+65) 6749-9343 Fax: (+65) 6749-9345 Email: singapore@rbc.org

Taiwan — RBC Ministries Foundation - PO Box 68-325 Taipei 104 Taiwan R.O.C.
Telephone: (+886-2) 254-17911 Fax: (+886-2) 252-39184 Email: taiwan@rbc.org

Thailand — RBC Ministries Thailand - PO Box 44 Hawkarnkhar University Bangkok 10325 Thailand
Telephone: (+66-2) 692-2476 Fax: (+66-2) 275-4467 Email: thailand@rbc.org

Philippines — RBC Ministries - PO Box 288 Greenhills 0410 Metro Manila, Philippines
Telephone: (+63-2) 722-2010 Fax: (+63-2) 725-5058 Email: philippines@rbc.org

Americas Region
Guyana — RBC Ministries - PO Box 101070 Georgetown Guyana
Telephone: (+592) 225-1428 Fax: (+592) 225-1428 Email: guyana@rbc.org

Jamaica — RBC Ministries - Box 123 Kingston 10 Jamaica
Telephone: (+876) 926-5765 Fax: (+876) 968-0747 Email: jamaica@rbc.org

Trinidad and Tobago — RBC Ministries - Corner Agostini & Belle Smythe Streets Curepe Trinidad and Tobago

USA (Regional Office) — RBC Ministries - PO Box 177 Grand Rapids MI 49501-0177 USA
Telephone: (+1-616) 954-1292 Fax: (+1-616) 957 5741 Email: literature@rbc.org (Spanish) imo@rbc.org (English)

Europe Region
United Kingdom (Regional Office) — RBC Ministries Europe - PO Box 1 Carnforth Lancashire LA5 9ES England
Telephone: (+1-524) 733-166 Fax: (+1-524) 736-194 Email: england@rbc.org